A-Z of Dinosaurs

Kieron Connolly

amber
BOOKS

Copyright © 2018 Amber Books Ltd

All rights reserved. No part of this publication may be reproduced, stored in a retrieval system, or transmitted in any form or by any means, electronic, mechanical, photocopying, recording, or otherwise, without prior written permission of the copyright holder.

Published by
Amber Books Ltd
United House
North Road
London
N7 9DP
United Kingdom
www.amberbooks.co.uk
Appstore: itunes.com/apps/amberbooksltd
Facebook: www.facebook.com/amberbooks
Twitter: @amberbooks

ISBN: 978-1-78274-564-8

Project Editor: Sarah Uttridge
Design: Keren Harragan and Andrew Easton

All artworks © IMP AB

Printed in China

Contents

6	Apatosaurus	19	Nodosaurus
7	Brachiosaurus	20	Ornitholestes
8	Carnotaurus	21	Protoceratops
9	Dimetrodon	22	Quetzalcoatlus
10	Edmontonia	23	Riojasaurus
11	Fulgurotherium	24	Stegosaurus
12	Gracilisuchus	25	Tyrannosaurus rex
13	Hypacrosaurus	26	Utahraptor
14	Iguanodon	27	Velociraptor
15	Jaxartosaurus	28	Wuerhosaurus
16	Kentrosaurus	29	Xiphactinus
17	Liliensternus	30	Yaverlandia
18	Maiasaura	31	Zephyrosaurus

Aa Apatosaurus

uh-PAT-uh-SAWR-us

The name means 'Misleading lizard'.

Tail
Apatosaurus had a long tail, which cracked like a whip when flicked.

Teeth
It had two rows of teeth for tearing leaves, but couldn't chew.

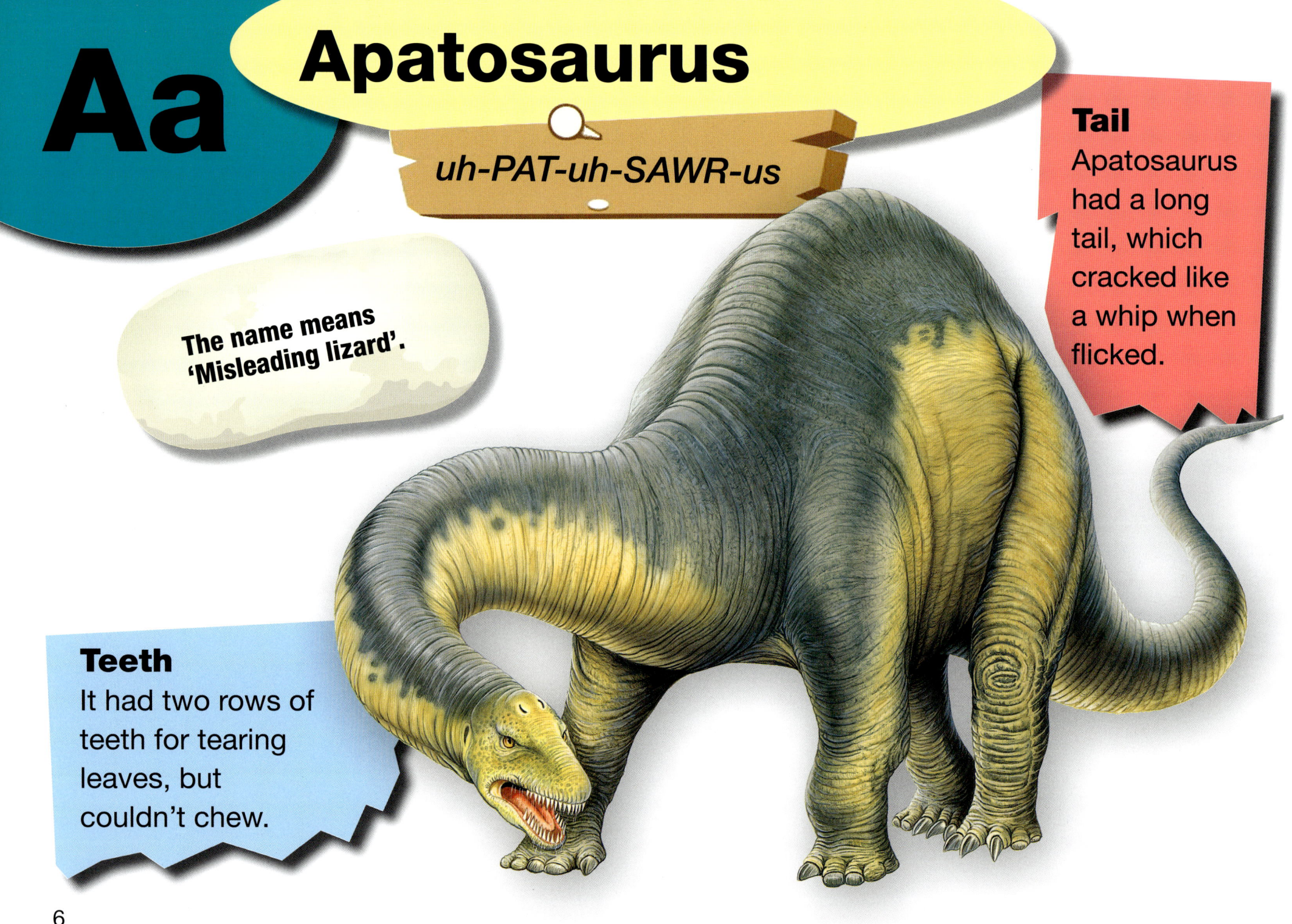

Brachiosaurus

BRACK-ee-uh-SAWR-us

Bb

The name means 'arm reptile'.

Legs
Its legs were thick and powerful to carry its heavy body.

Neck
Brachiosaurus' long neck helped it feed from high trees.

Cc Carnotaurus

car-no-TAWR-us

The name means 'meat-eating bull'.

Eyes
Carnotaurus' eyes faced forward. This helped it tell how far away things were.

Scales
Its tough skin was covered in small scales.

Dimetrodon

Dd

dy-MEE-tro-don

The name means 'two-measures of teeth'.

Sail
The great fin on its back helped it stay balanced.

Teeth
Dimetrodon had two kinds of teeth: some for cutting and some for ripping meat apart.

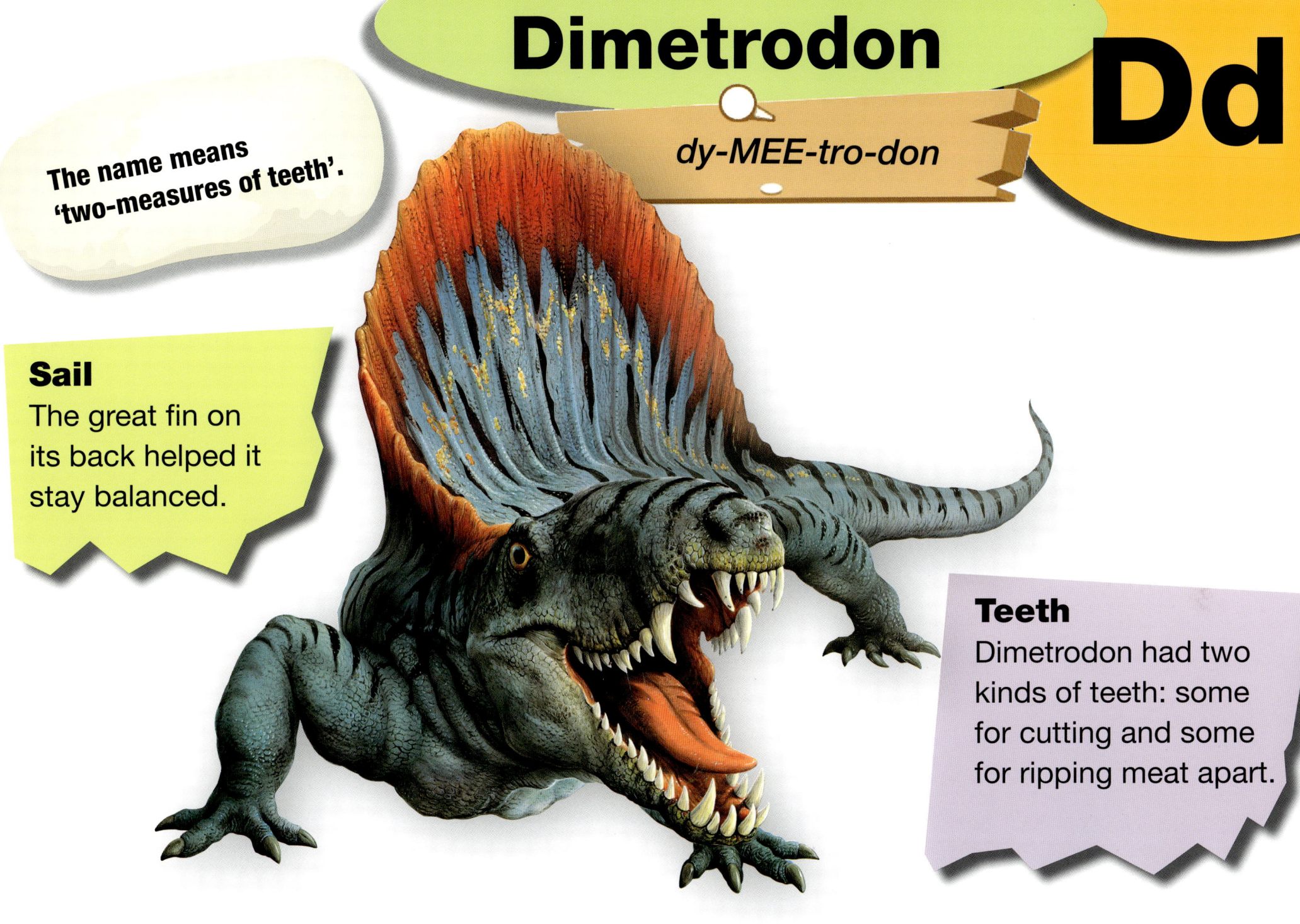

Ee Edmontonia

ed-mon-TOE-nee-ah

It was named after Edmonton Rock Formation in Canada, where it was found.

Armour
The back was protected by plates made of bone.

Beak
Edmontonia had a beak and a few simple teeth at the back of its jaw.

Fulgurotherium

Ff

FUL-gur-o-THEER-ee-um

The name means 'Lightning beast'.

Legs
Fulgurotherium ran quickly on two legs.

Cheeks
It stored chewed-up plant food in its cheeks.

Gg Gracilisuchus

GRAS-i-li-SOOK-us

The name means 'slim crocodile'.

Plates
Gracilisuchus was protected by bony plates all down its back.

Jaws
It caught prey with its huge jaws.

Hypacrosaurus

Hi-PACK-roe-SAWR-us

Hh

The name means 'Almost the top lizard'.

Teeth
Hypacrosaurus had 40 rows of teeth to grind up plants and fruit.

Length
Its body was 9 metres (30 feet long).

Ii

Iguanodon

Ig-WAHN-oh-don

The name means 'Iguana tooth'.

Thumb
Iguanodon had a spike like a thumb sticking out from each hand.

Stomach
It needed a large, long stomach to digest all the plants it ate.

Jaxartosaurus

Jax-SAHR-toh-SAWR-us

Jj

Crest
Scientists believe it used the air passages in the crest of its head to make a trumpeting sound.

The name means 'Jaxartes lizard', after the Jaxartes river in Kazakhstan.

Legs
Jaxartosaurus mainly stood on four legs but could rise onto its back legs if necessary.

Kk Kentrosaurus

KEN-troh-SAWR-us

The name means 'Spiked lizard'.

Nose
Kentrosaurus had a very strong sense of smell.

Legs
It could stand on its back legs.

Liliensternus

LIL-ee-in-STERN-us

It was named after the palaeontologist (a scientist who studies fossils) Hugo Rühle von Lilienstern.

Hands
Its hands had five fingers. The first and fifth fingers were smaller than the central ones.

Hunter
Lilensternus lived in forests and on riverbanks, and hunted in packs.

Ll

Mm Maiasaura

My-uh-SAWR-uh

The name means 'Good mother lizard'.

Teeth
When its teeth wore out, they were replaced by more teeth moving forward.

Beak
Maiasaura had a wide duck-like beak with strong muscular jaws.

Nodosaurus

No-doe-SAWR-us

The name means 'Knob lizard'.

Armour
Nodosaurus had thick bony plates on its back to protect it against predators.

Discovery
It was one of the first armoured dinosaurs to be discovered in North America.

Oo Ornitholestes

or-NITH-oh-LESS-teez

The name means 'Bird robber'.

Height
Ornitholestes was only 30 centimetres (12 inches high).

Thumb
The third finger acted like a thumb, allowing it to grip.

Protoceratops

Pp

Proh-toh-SEH-ratops

The name means 'First horn face'.

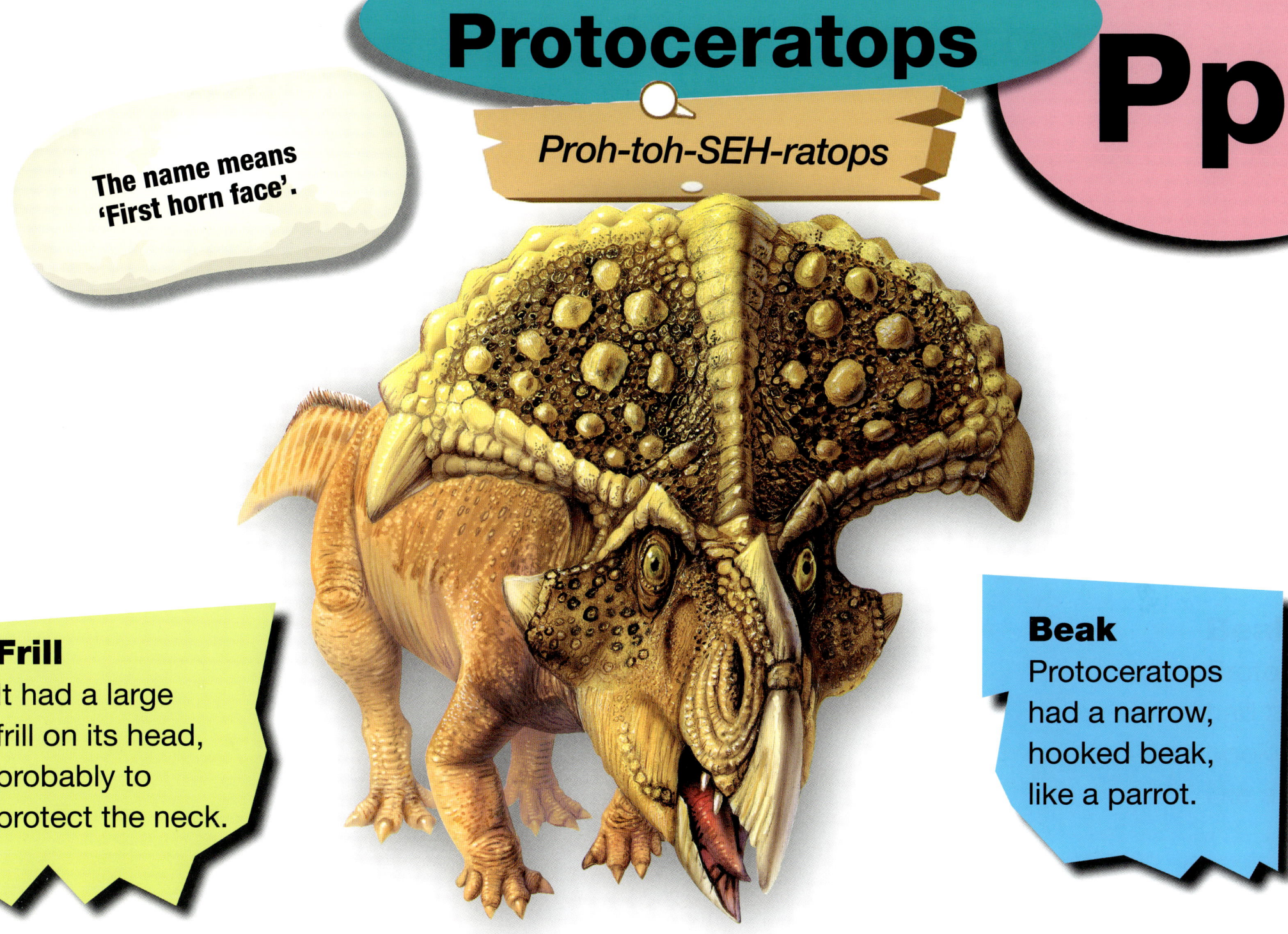

Frill
It had a large frill on its head, probably to protect the neck.

Beak
Protoceratops had a narrow, hooked beak, like a parrot.

Qq Quetzalcoatlus

Kett-zal-coe-AT-luss

The name means 'Plumed serpent'.

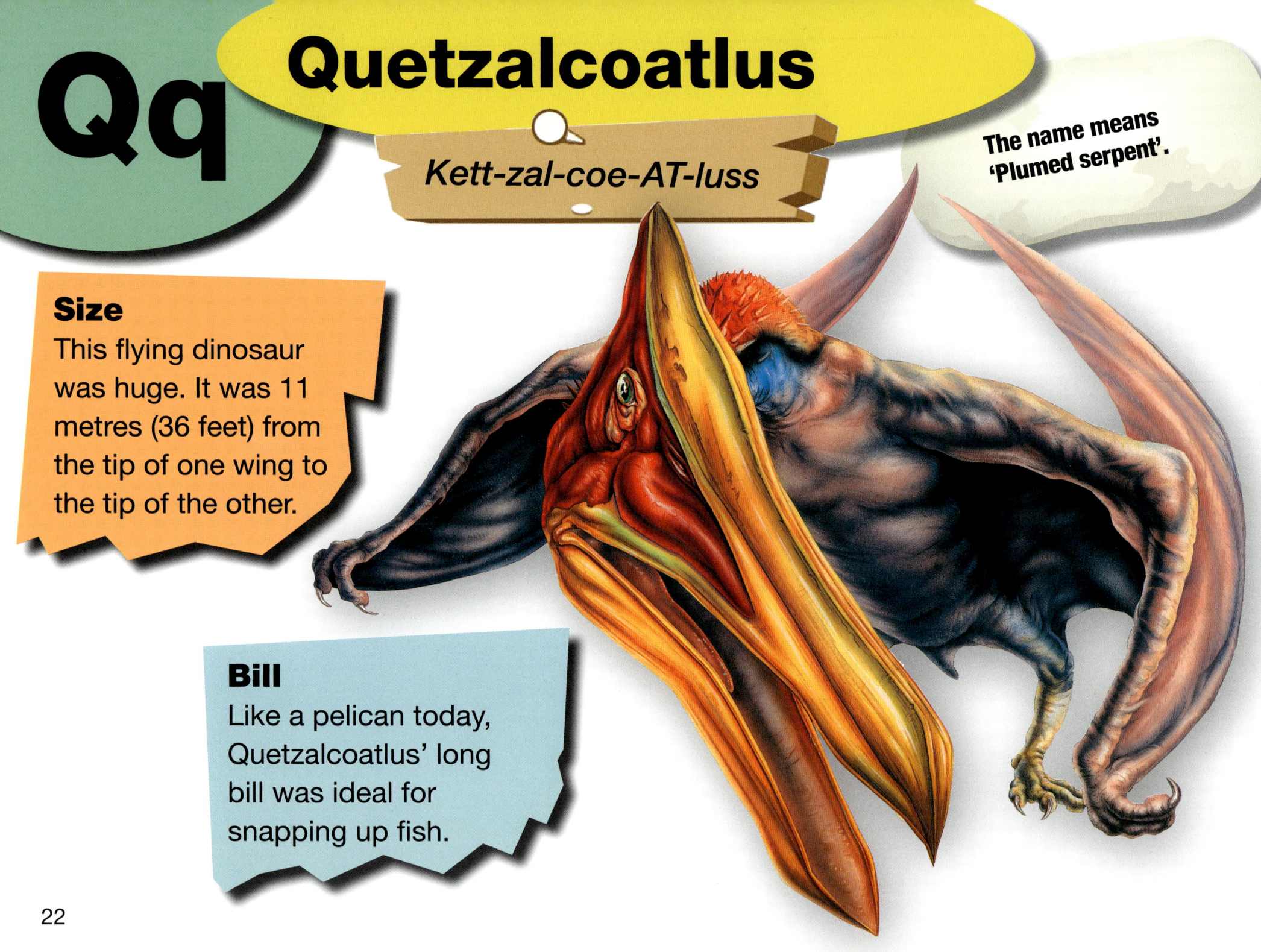

Size
This flying dinosaur was huge. It was 11 metres (36 feet) from the tip of one wing to the tip of the other.

Bill
Like a pelican today, Quetzalcoatlus' long bill was ideal for snapping up fish.

Riojasaurus

Ree-OH-ha-SAWR-us

Rr

The name means 'Rioja lizard'.

Tail
Its long tail helped it balance.

Brain
Riojasaurus had a very big body. It was 5 metres (16 feet) tall but had a very small brain.

Ss Stegosaurus

STEG-oh-SAWR-us

The name means 'Roofed lizard'.

Plates
The plates on its back were made of bone.

Spikes
It is believed that these spikes were used as a weapon.

Tyrannosaurus rex

Tye-RAN-oh-sawr-us rex

Tt

The name means 'King tyrant lizard'.

Weight
Tyrannosaurus rex weighed 700 kilograms (7 tons).

Teeth
It had bigger teeth than any other meat-eating dinosaur.

Uu Utahraptor

YU-tar-RAP-tor

Head It had a large head containing a large brain.

The name means 'Utah thief'.

Claw The curved claw stuck upward. It was used for attacking prey.

Velociraptor

Vv

VEL-ossi-RAP-tor

The name means 'Speedy thief'.

Teeth
Velociraptor had 28 teeth on each side of its jaw.

Tail
Its tail was almost twice as long as its body.

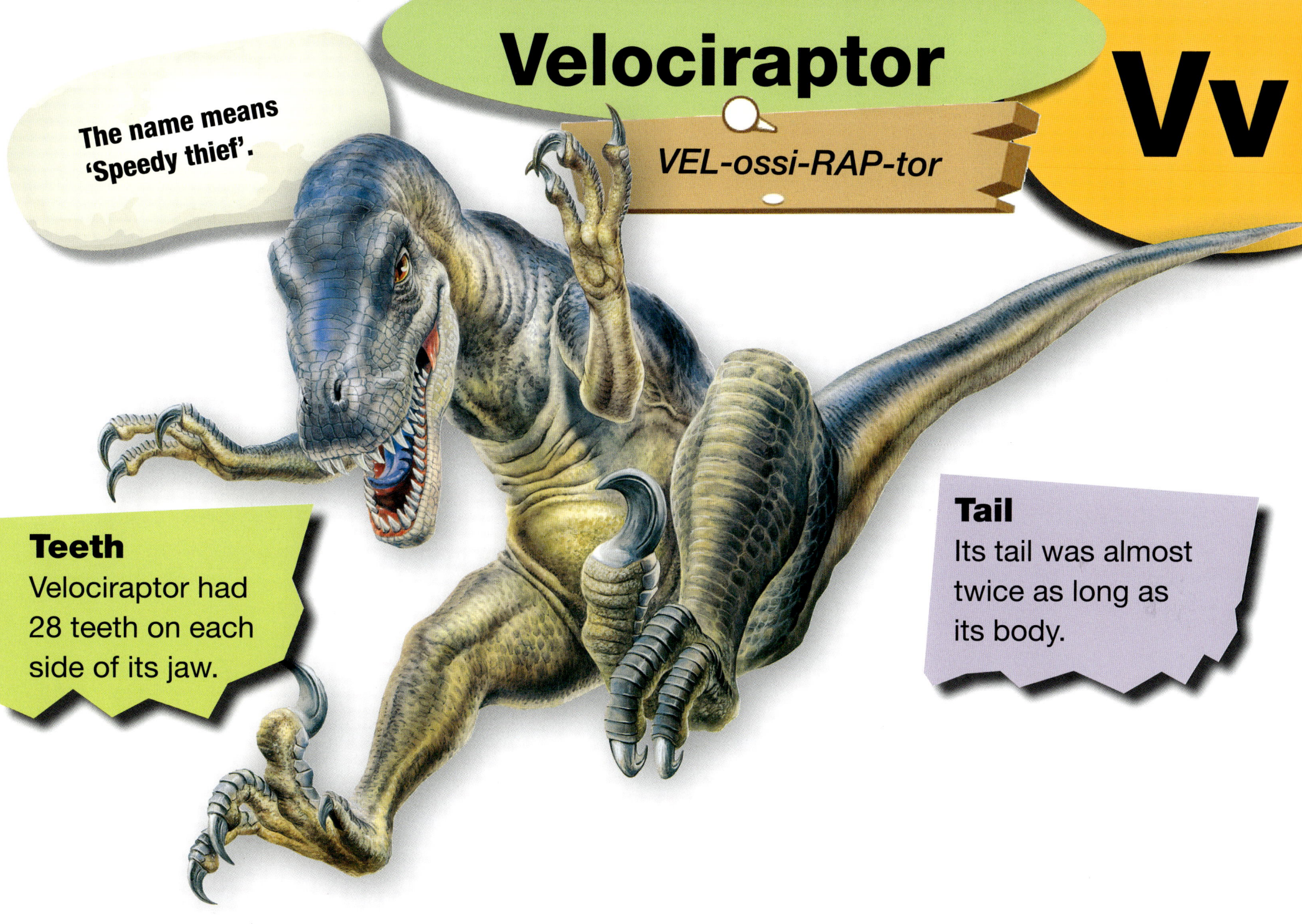

Ww Wuerhosaurus

Woo-AYR-hoh-SAWR-us

The name means 'Wuerho lizard'.

Plates
Unlike other dinosaurs, its plates were rectangular, not triangular.

Spikes
Scientists believe the tail was flicked around to throw the spikes against attackers.

Xiphactinus

zy-FACT-in-us

Xx

The name means 'Sword ray'.

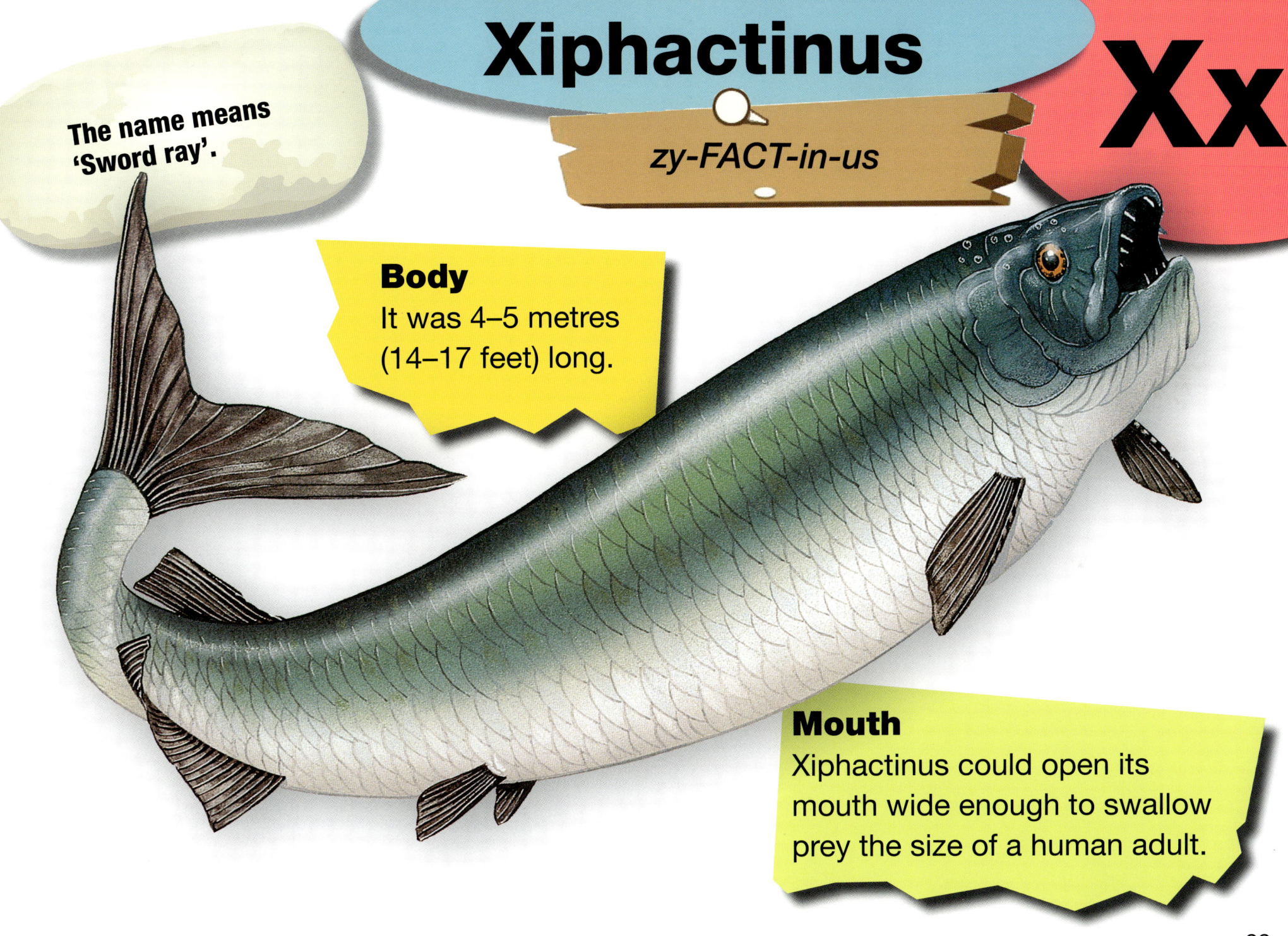

Body
It was 4–5 metres (14–17 feet) long.

Mouth
Xiphactinus could open its mouth wide enough to swallow prey the size of a human adult.

Yy

Yaverlandia

Yah-ver-LAN-dee-ah

The name means 'From Yaverland'.

Head
Yaverlandia had two domes at the front of its head. Scientists believe these were used in fights.

Hands
Scientists think it had long arms and hands with three fingers.

Zephyrosaurus

Zz

ZEF-i-ro-SAWR-us

The name means 'West wind lizard'.

Legs
Zephyrosaurus had long back legs that allowed it to run quickly.

Teeth
It could not only move its jaws up and down but also side to side, helping it eat.

31

Aa
Apatosaurus
uh-PAT-uh-SAWR-us

Bb
Brachiosaurus
BRACK-ee-uh-SAWR-us

Cc
Carnotaurus
car-no-TAWR-us

Dd
Dimetrodon
dy-MEE-tro-don

Ee
Edmontonia
ed-mon-TOE-nee-ah

Ff
Fulgurotherium
FUL-gur-o-THEER-ee-um

Gg
Gracilisuchus
GRAS-i-li-SOOK-us

Hh
Hypacrosaurus
Hi-PACK-roe-SAWR-us

Ii
Iguanodon
Ig-WAHN-oh-don

Jj
Jaxartosaurus
Jax-SAHR-toh-SAWR-us

Kk
Kentrosaurus
KEN-troh-SAWR-us

Ll
Liliensternus
LIL-ee-in-STERN-us

Mm
Maiasaura
My-uh-SAWR-uh

Nn
Nodosaurus
No-doe-SAWR-us

Oo
Ornitholestes
or-NITH-oh-LESS-teez

Pp
Protoceratops
Proh-toh-SEH-ratops

Qq
Quetzalcoatlus
Kett-zal-coe-AT-luss

Rr
Riojasaurus
Ree-OH-ha-SAWR-us

Ss
Stegosaurus
STEG-oh-SAWR-us

Tt
Tyrannosaurus rex
Tye-RAN-oh-sawr-us rex

Uu
Utahraptor
YU-tar-RAP-tor

Vv
Velociraptor
VEL-ossi-RAP-tor

Ww
Wuerhosaurus
Woo-AYR-hoh-SAWR-us

Xx
Xiphactinus
zy-FACT-in-us

Yy
Yaverlandia
Yah-ver-LAN-dee-ah

Zz
Zephyrosaurus
ZEF-i-ro-SAWR-us